Writing over the
word limit

McKenna Graf

BookLeaf
Publishing

writing over the word limit © 2023
McKenna Graf

Presentation by *BookLeaf Publishing*

Web: www.bookleafpub.com

E-mail: info@bookleafpub.com

ISBN: 9789357440004

First edition 2023

dedication

To the several versions of me who doubted I could ever get here, I proved you wrong.

acknowledgement

I would like to thank BookLeaf Publishing for giving aspiring writers like myself this incredible opportunity to get our work published. I would like to thank everyone who helped me in the publishing process after I completed the initial challenge of writing the poems. I would like to thank my boyfriend at the time for supporting me and tirelessly editing with me. I would like to thank my friends and cousins for looking at and workshopping 10 or more different versions of the title and cover, ultimately giving in and supporting my passion for writing. And I of course would like to thank my family who I very humbly told I was participating in this and they got extremely excited for me when I was too scared to. Thank you to everyone for believing in me when I couldn't or was scared to believe in myself. I hope there is something in my words that speaks to each of you as my way of saying thank you for reading.

preface

Queer, awkward and often in love. "writing over the word limit" is my debut poetry collection of expressing oneself and a desire to grow despite all odds or limitations.

So light a candle, get comfy, and spend an hour getting lost in my words and I hope you'll find something worth continuing to think about beyond the time we spend together.

flowers can grow in the cracks of the sidewalk

I'm typing in the dark.
    My friend said it sounds like rain
        drops falling on the
                ground.
Keys pressed down together
in the cover of night.
Most things are possible,
like telling you a fairytale
and you taking it for truth
or reading you a poem
of my own
when in the light
reciting makes it
hard to breathe. The
stars at night are hiding
pockets of breath in between lines and
giving me the bravery to try when
I'm afraid you'll think it's dry. I
oftentimes fill the moon with tears
but in the inbetween,
the magic of the moment
before falling asleep,
I find myself with
poems dripping from my ear
and sliding off the pillow
until it colors my journal page with

scrawled black ink,
eyes that see beyond
and a mind that awakes when it's meant
to sleep.

stuck in quicksand

I get mad easily
and deny myself
easier.
They used to make
me the villain
because I got the
temper gene
    times two.
And I hate being criticized.
I wish I could make my
(voice quieter).
I get yelled at for
being too loud
even when I'm
not mad.
It's like
no matter what I do
I'm too much of a person,
  feel too much,
    see too much,
and reactions bubble and
                  boil
                    over the surface.

It hurts that
even still I'm getting burned
because I'm using tone
and I need to be

COMPOSED.
I taught myself
that
blowing up wasn't ok
so rolling it up inside
and tying it up with a bow
is how it must go.
Presentation is key.
I suppose there's an inbetween
but I don't think I'll ever know.

sweating in the cold, this is getting old

Self-sacrificing,
always waiting for someone to
accidentally
notice I let them
forget what was
on my mind.
Lost shoes in Italy
and so many books
I'll never find.
If I could rewind
I'd let myself
speak my mind,
but not in defense,
simply a request.
The worst would
be it denied
but I never
give it a try.
So either way
I'll cry
but leave the sob
choked in the
back of my
         throat
            (and mind),
trapped behind padded doors,
there's no room anymore.

But I don't deserve the release
when I never even
gave my thoughts space to breathe.

hyper aware of you there

I set these impossible standards
for myself
because I'm the oldest.
Now somehow I'm the coldest.
I cripple with anxiety
when I fall short of the
standards I've set for me.
I don't know how to live
for myself
when I'm always thinking about
someone else.
I wipe out while I'm skiing and I'm
stuck on perception.
A more bruised EGO than
any physical pain
because
the one time you set a
standard for me as,
"*She's so great at skiing!*"
I wore that skin proudly
and crashed.
The emotional wall cracked.
I put too much value in
living up to me in your head but
all these standards are bullshit and,
I'd like to spread my wings and
go sit on a mushroom for a while.

maybe learn how to
prioritize my smile.

I take on too much responsibility sometimes

I'm ripping my heart out
and the sun is cracking the sky into
pieces.
The pressure is pushing my head into
my heart
and I'm not sure which way is up.
My eyes spin around the room
and I've suddenly grown ten extra hands.
The horizon keeps me grounded and
I'm crawling around
on the floor
for my glasses
even though I could
see the whole time.

don't talk back (god forbid we replied and were right)

I think it's interesting for you
to say it's hard to break
this habit,
but a habit of
picking your nails or cursing
you'll work hard to break.
When it's convenient for you
sure that's something you can do
but when you need to think for one

extra second
the younger generation is
asking too much of you.
But you're the ones putting the
weight of the world heating
on their back
and throwing sexist stereotypes in their faces
of which no one should have to conform.
But you love your form and
order
and
uniform,
and anything that's a step

                                             outside

is too hard
for you.

It must be so hard for you to
wake up in the morning without your coffee
and get your parking spot stolen.
You let your boss call you the wrong name
because you're too afraid to speak up.
Maybe then you'd understand how
the young feel
when they correct
and you still don't respect.
You make everyone who dares to stand
out

                                    stand

alone,
and offer no branch on which for them to stand.
Boxing them [in] from the start,
a creation that has fostered such hatred,
because you claim it hurts
your vocabulary.
When all they did was ask
     plead
and you said they SCREAMED,
for one single word,
one blanketing phrase
to make one feel safe.
It was just out of
                    reach,
outside of the bubble you created
that you thought was safe for yourself,
but not

for the ones poked and prodded
because you won't let them
out.
Forcing them inside a skin,

        a name,

          a body,

that is not theirs.
But of course
it's not difficult on them
when you use the wrong pronouns
because it's harder on you

       "it's a habit I just can't break"

and you just assumed.
But what happened to assuming
making an ass (out of) u (and) me,

       like my dad said.

You shove them back into
a skin they don't want
that they worked so hard to remold like clay
and somehow you still find the scraps
and shove it back down their throats
and

       there's something wrong with me

coughs up their lungs.
When it is entirely a problem with
a STUBBORN SOCIETY
that refuses all we can be,
the lines that can be blurred
and skies that can be burned.

There is no limit to what
we can do or be.
There is no limit to what
we can't break.
They say it's hard and
we must wait
but I see an ocean of waves
that we can make.
There are battles to be fought
but not at the cost
of your precious soul.
We will walk down this path TOGETHER
and find the flowers on the way
that transform your bouquet,
that make it seem like soon
this will be ok
and we will have a say.
You say enough's been done,
Why do you clamor for more?
I reply why do you treat us like
a problem to be fixed?

       (*hush little baby, here's your bottle*
       if we are babies to you, expect a trojan
horse   )

there is not just one demographic to represent
despite what you see behind your white picket
fence.

I must be spelling selfish wrong

My therapist reminded me that
the mother puts on her oxygen mask
before her child's.
She said
it's important
that you take care of yourself
before you even begin to
take care of others.
Ripping out everything you have
in the hopes that one
effort isn't futile
that it
brings a friend a smile,
but it's like telling a washing machine
to run with no detergent in.
You're
          throwing
      them   around
        in   their
           tears,
but nothing can be healed
or washed,
because your hands are
not clean.
They're stained in blood
from ripping out a heart
that is barely even beating,
from pulling out (hair) that's
no longer there.
Your face is covered in

STRESS PIMPLES
that will never go away
if you keep valuing
THEIR needs
and stepping on your own.

I drew tarot cards with my friends
and my future was death.
I thought it meant the end
of me or something important to me
when it actually meant
shedding this toxic identity.

numbing cream

I scream
in my mind
all the time
but it never hits my lips.
It sticks with this phrase that
I don't deserve being heard.
My heart plastered in a mold
so my pieces don't pierce anyone else.
To myself I drill a narrative
that is more damaging
than the hurt of the world
because I can get knocked down
but there's always a way to get up,
a

     p
  h   o
    o
  l   l   e

I don't know.
but my mind tells me
I don't deserve to know.
I'm not allowed to grab the
outstretched hand,
the concerns of a loved one.
And I'm trying so hard to
let myself do so,
but I'm so used to
refusing the help.
I hear the phrase repeated

"you're acting like a victim crying when it's not about you."
A phrase that may be fabricated
from a fight I can't shake off,
but a phrase rooted in my veins.
I'd rather succumb to my own poison
than let anyone else
be infected by what
weighs down my heart.
So I don't cry it out
I let the sob lodge in my throat.
It's better they don't know,
they'd be better off without.

You say, *"you know that's not true"*
I reply, *"but it's a killing habit I don't know
how to live without."*

holding up the sky and I don't know why

The female experience
is being taught that
you can't say no.
You're taking too much for yourself
that belongs to a man.
Don't you see his name right there?
scribbled in red on the left?

"Don't just stand there,
bring me a can
of beer
won't you dear?"

No sweet smile
just sick teeth
and poisoned words
and we still let them
bite into
our shoulders and minds.
We never ask him to get us
wine
or beer.
We'd never whine
because time has told us,

"You're nothing without a man
so don't upset him,
you're lucky he chose you
otherwise you'll never get ahead,

So why do you even try?"

My grandma's guidance counselor
told her she could never be a nurse,
a curse that killed her dream.
Another silenced plea.

Fuck that guy.

russian nesting dolls

I'm creating new versions
of myself everyday
Chasing the future
when I should stay
and drink in the day
where new moments pass
me by
if I'm sitting here
worrying why,
I do this
and she does that.
It's too easy to say I'll
turn off my phone
and just not look.
It's harder to
{embrace}
that everyone does what
suits them best
and so should the rest.
I am of a generation
of instant gratification
and comparison,
but of the generation to
make the most change
as we
accept ourselves and
hold each other's hands.

I am creating me
everyday

so that there is a day
I can confidently hold
those hands
and help as we pave
a new way.

my heart beats

I don't know if I'll ever get
on that stage
but I know you'll see
my name on that page.
I may not have all the
pieces
but I see so many faces
and places
that are calling my name
begging to be written down.
And I do not know the plan,
I don't need to be the best
or have the most detailed road
map,
I just want this to be the rest
of MY life.
Lighting candles
and igniting stories.

I want to be the one you're
(holding).
I want to dance in the mist
and kiss the stars
and let my tongue
                    drip
ink and then
                the stories

                        will write
themselves.

I want to MAKE
something to be proud of.
I want to take
off the skin of
the people pleaser
RIP
      SHRED
                  SLICE
it int
      o
pieces,
so I can wear my scars proud
and be clad in the skin of my HEART,
         "*she is not perfect*
                  but she is mine"
and I've accidentally quoted Waitress
but who am I but not an
amalgamation of all the art
in the world
seeking to make my own MARK
and light a path
for the young,
                  confused,
                              and alone
for a start,

I'd like to join the (alphabet) mafia

Messy little handwriting
and big boxed thoughts.
It's [brackets upon brackets]
of a storm
            of unorganized chaos,
of a swarm
            of never-ending thoughts,
and pots
and pans
and why am I staring at your hands?
And why do I want to be holding them?
These thoughts are holding
and molding
and I melt
and I melt
and I me
            l
            t
whoiamiscompressed
into ONE tiny word,
in scrawled letters
(in the margins).
Because there was no
camera on more than
him and her
and him and him
and you and you. And

in a world full of
modeling after the media
how was I supposed to know
there was more inside me.
See,
there's plenty of fish in the sea
but I want to stop
and meet
all the souls in garden
and be allowed to
have your hand be the
only one I'm holding
and never questioned why
or placed back in the box
we'd just be,

coming out feels more like battling homophobia than being myself

I've been writing out of
anger,
a temper I
inherited from my parents
because
I've been writing to
find a way for the ones
that are constantly shamed
for trying to feel ok
in their own skin.
Because
I know I've
never wanted to
crawl out of my skin
out of disgust
more than
when I say
I'd prefer the princess
over the prince and
all I get are
blank stares.
They accept me as
one of them
because
I like all
so I like
men.
But when they remember
the

all
part of myself
I can
no longer hang
with them.
I have a boyfriend
so I'm acceptable
but saying I'd
prefer Meg
over Hercules
is
                    too far.
It's interesting because
you have no problem when
men choose men
to a point that it
feels like a fetish,
but when a
girl kisses a girl
you don't like it.
Shows get canceled
and
books go unread.
It's WILD.
I think
if you hadn't dismissed the
sexy sapphics
as less
            than
maybe I'd have a
role model
to realize that

I was like them
sooner than
the end of
high school;
latching onto a show
so hard my
knuckles turn white.
Because this is in favor of women
and it won't stay for long.
I must hold on tight
to them who make me feel safe
so they'll stay just a little longer
before I see the bolded word,
CANCELED.
And I wonder
how many more
closeted girls
will suffer for that decision
and sew up that part of themselves
with practiced precision.

wednesday addams is queer

Why is it so impossible for
some to sit and enjoy
anything beyond the norm?
Any deviation from the
creation
of years of oppression of differences.
And you've got your panties in a twist
because I would kiss a girl
and suddenly the world's toes
curl.
And yet I'm forced to
announce it to the world
so I'm not assumed
the stereotype.
Why does it matter to you who I like?
And why do you think
there's only one? Like
you taste all the cheeses
until you find the one you like.
Why is a statement that simply means
OPEN TO EXPLORE
such a shocking revelation
when there's such a
constant separation
between boy and girl.
He screams I have
cooties
and she's inviting me
to her house to play
barbies.

Is it that surprising
that someone who
hates all men
wouldn't simply
swear off them,
but move onto
women?

And those who look inside,
it's not the ones they like
that makes them
"different"
but it's inside that's been
shifting,
signaling everytime
a pronoun is used
that somethings
being abused.
The self is delicate
and precious
and often wrapped up
into a name or a
phrase
and many toss
                    it
into the
                        wind
like it doesn't have the
power to invalidate
the self you've created.
I see the worlds
you've been creating

and the self
you've been making
and it's time to start

    H
S   A   G
    K   N
         I

until the world falls upside
down.
I am so immensely proud
of everyone listening to and
advocating for themselves.
A plant can't grow without
water
just as you can't grow without
loving yourself.
But it always helps
to feel loved.

So allow me to be the one
to sprinkle pixie dust
in the clouds
and spread the love
all around with
a constant phrase,
I AM PROUD
of every version of you
especially the one that
thought they couldn't be brave.
You saved
yourself from the
pain of denial.

And for the ones still
struggling to smile,
there may seem to be
a thousand miles ahead
but at least in me you have a friend
and there is no end
to my love and pride.
We can take that next stride
and it may be a long ride,
but I'll be there by your side.
Because we are not the odd one out,
we infiltrate every crowd,
and our voices will be heard loud.
So don't dismiss us when we say
a character is queer,
we need some role model
to tell us it's safe.

my childhood blanket was ripped into pieces

I can't romanticize New Jersey,
not in the way one can with New England.
But maybe when I dive into
my childhood home,
the trees surrounding the
property like a blanket.
The highways we made out of
chalk on the driveway
thinking they could take us
anywhere.
Here is where we made
lemonade stands with
water,
grandma gave us pancakes
made out of cardboard so
we could play house.
There's the tree we learned to climb,
but most often learned how to fall.
The pool we learned to float
and the house where we learned to love.
There's a
million memories
simmering behind those walls
waiting for us to touch and
let it be released.
There's a
million memories
it never got to see
and I imagine it weeps

for the versions of us
it never got to see.
My childhood lives in those
pink walls and
hardwood floors.
I would give anything to
go back again
and feel that
shaggy blue carpet beneath
my feet and
in between my toes.
But I know
I've come too far to
go backwards again.
I've learned how to
make real pancakes
and drive on real highways.
I'm taking myself to actual places,
I'm finding real jobs and
finding spaces where I belong
beyond those pink walls
that I thought could keep me safe.
It's funny I
used to hide in my closet when
the voices in my head got too loud.
I think little me would be proud that
I've stepped out of the closet and
am working on
wearing my skin and emotions with pride.

walking through the underworld

hope the fates hold the string
of my life as delicately
as I'd want my love to hold me.
Because I want a love like the gods,
more powerful than
anything else.
Like a florence and the machines song,
big GODS
selfishly sipping ambrosia
out of a never
ending tea cup.
Mortals would erect
altars for our kind of love,
sucking your thumb
just to get a taste of you
like a bee to
honey,
you're my achilles heel.
I'd die over
and over
again for you.
You're the light that I fly too
close
        to
every greek tragedy and
great love
wrapped into ONE.
You're my immortality,
I covet you
like egotistical greek heroes do,

35

and I've been thinking
about how
mountains make me
feel existential
       (which you know scares me)
and yet are essential
to this idea of
seeing
words hidden
                under
            the trees,
or written in the
veins of the leaves,
or glistening so bright
                  in the snow.
No words come quicker
or make me sit with them longer,
they linger
in this existential feeling
of words coming without my permission,
their slipping in the back of my brain
and then taking over my eyes.
I see them and
suddenly the backdrop is the world
to this performance of words
and the only times
I feel it stronger
are
   laughing,
          talking,
             kissing
YOU.

But mostly
looking at
        you,
your eyes are like a
deep chocolate river.
I fall into its thickness
but I swim in its richness
and it's lighter than I've ever felt before.
I like to dream of them
when your eyes are closed
and the words come from the
sparks that light up
your face
when you open them for me.
It's like little blips in my
string of life
where I feel I reach some
paradise
and that moment in my string of life
grows brighter.
There are times where it feels like
it's dragging on the floor
tangled in the depths of tartarus
and sometimes
I don't know how to climb it,
I don't have great upper body strength,
and
I'm afraid of heights.
Sometimes I'll just wade

                                out

into the darkness and
        veer

                    off   the
path   of
                                    the
string.
but then I end up on
another,
because different choices
take us to different timelines
and somehow,
I get back to a bright spot.
I get back to you.
because no matter what
timeline I stumble into,
I'll always fall into
you.
And the bright spots will follow
too
(because they're mostly
you)
and before the fates cut our
string,
I hope to tear through
all the dark with you.
Because it's not so dark
with my bright spot
by my side.
Your soul has been tied
to mine
and I'm so glad I found
the loose thread
tying yours to mine
and did not turn around too soon,

but walked forward
and found you at that desk,
found you by my side.
I've got glasses
for a reason my love
(I couldn't see)
but I had my epic love all along.
It was just inside
knocking to the tune
I didn't yet know the name of but
it was your name and mine,
and I've always felt a
tickle of a word
on the tip of my tongue,
and it's been yours
the whole time.

it's three you see

You said to
write about infinity,
how it stands for
you and me.
You say that
cut in half
it's made up of
two 3's.
3 has always been
significant to us,
separately,
I don't know how it
came to be
but we have all these
coincidences,
(coincidences)
(coincidences)
stacked upon one another.
Almost touching
and just

       missing
a declaration at the
end of our tongues.
Moments we had
but didn't understand.
it took 3 seconds
to grab your face
and press your
lips to mine
after 3 years of

repressed longing,
I hid.
Because loving you meant
there was something different
in me.
I'm not fond of change
but you've held my
hand in yours
          (and let our fingertips dance)
all this time
saying,
          "it's just me,"
amidst a thousand butterflies
          (that split in half
                          also make two 3's)
circling my stomach
that I refused to name.
I don't know why it
took me
so
long
to see my blushing face
and your name always
circling in my mind,
but,
thank you for
being patient with me
until I saw the line
that's been
standing right in front of me.
And then with your hand
walked on confidently,

taking me to the
infinity of you and me.

fairytale of me

I'm sloughing off
                    the skin
of my old self,
wondering how I didn't
(suffocate).
Proud that I found some
way to advocate
for myself. I
always think that
thinking of me first is
selfish
but it's different when
I've never
done that before.
I would
fall on the floor
to meet your needs and
overcompensate in my interests
because they were your interests
and maybe then you'd have some,
interest in me.
but I've ripped off that skin
(my skin was like a blanket
            my shield
                    that's why I rip it off so much)
and painted my nails
        (who knew choosing the color
            that I want
                became a new type of skin
                    like the skin of a selkie

43

expressing who I am)
I think one day
I'd like to
try on a mermaid tail and fairy wings,
and I'm not afraid to share that.
I'm learning not to care about your
perception of me.
I'm sinking my feet into
the earth
and
diving into the sea,
untamed and unknown,
I will be nothing but myself,
a mystery, I'll be
collecting seashells
if it pleases me.

spilt ink

I sometimes worry I have
nothing important to say,
that no matter how hard
I pull at my hair
gold strands won't come out.
I can't make myself rumpelstiltskin
by injecting his talents into my veins
or declaring it's my turn to
change the world,
words have power
but an intention must be set.
And I was once told
I wasn't tortured enough
to be a writer,
      to be a writer,
to be a writer is not about torture
or being driven mad by the words spiraling inside.
I already have glasses
I don't need to let the ink claim my sight.
my fingers they may claim
but I've learned to see the
                      inbetween.
That I can trudge through the darkness
and let it stick to my fingerprints
and bottle the light in my hand
and blow it all on the page.
But the biggest thing I can spark
is a passion for what I write
rather than stilted dedication to writing everyday.
I have something to say,

I twist and turn and suck on words
like a kernel until they feel right.
I want to feel so much in this life
to transcribe onto the page,
so that my tears and fears seep
in these years of pages and

pages

and stages of
writing so much that my whole life
has been written in crappy sonnets and
run-on sentences,
detailing every moment I panicked, loved, or
celebrated.
Maybe it's a stupid thing to think
but, words bring me comfort and calm
and I want that serenity to live on,
to store it in someone's pocket,
to burrow in the crevices of their complex brain
when they need a quote to explain,
it's hard living if there's no words to express all that's
swarming inside.

It steadies the storm and parts the clouds.
In some place my words will remain
but for now this page I will stain.

a fall's day

Academically I see
where words might need
to be set free.
But when
I'm expressing myself
don't confine me.
You can't shove this personality
into a tiny box because
it's too much for you.
I will always seep
out of the cracks
and latch onto the world.
We have too much to explore together
on the page
for you to pick at my
words
like a vulture.
I am not
pesky,
annoying,
allow me to refine on my own time
and not convince me I have,
too many thoughts,
when, where else but
on the page
should I write every
vein and string and root

of every thought and word that
ever crossed my mind?
My life has a limit
but my words do not.
I will write past arthritis
and until I go blind.
You can not
calm the
storm in my mind.
I will be here all the time,

21 divided by 7 is 3

This book is the
fantasy of a fifth grader.
A thousand connections
coincidences
and opportunities taken
brought us here.
The pages may grow dusty
and the cover worn away by the years
until it's all been burnt as
kindle to warm a heart,
a new purpose,
a new start.
But no matter the
new life it creates
in your hands,
it will beat
strongly
in my heart
as the one time I
decided to start
and give the world my
art.
It still has room to grow,
    I know,
but if I never plant the seed,
I can't reap what I
don't sow.
So let your hands that
turn the page
be the water for the ground

and your eyes on the page
be the light that helps it grow.
Close the book and
see it for the flower it is,
small but growing roots,
and I hope the world sees it soon.

Printed in the USA
CPSIA information can be obtained
at www.ICGtesting.com
LVHW052158190424
777952LV00009B/115

9 789357 440004